DOG BREEDS

Dalmatians

by Sara Green

Consultant:
Michael Leuthner, D.V.M.
Petcare Animal Hospital
Madison, Wisc.

BLASTOFF!
READERS
4

Note to Librarians, Teachers, and Parents:

Blastoff! Readers are carefully developed by literacy experts and combine standards-based content with developmentally appropriate text.

Level 1 provides the most support through repetition of high-frequency words, light text, predictable sentence patterns, and strong visual support.

Level 2 offers early readers a bit more challenge through varied simple sentences, increased text load, and less repetition of high-frequency words.

Level 3 advances early-fluent readers toward fluency through increased text and concept load, less reliance on visuals, longer sentences, and more literary language.

Level 4 builds reading stamina by providing more text per page, increased use of punctuation, greater variation in sentence patterns, and increasingly challenging vocabulary.

Level 5 encourages children to move from "learning to read" to "reading to learn" by providing even more text, varied writing styles, and less familiar topics.

Whichever book is right for your reader, Blastoff! Readers are the perfect books to build confidence and encourage a love of reading that will last a lifetime!

This edition first published in 2011 by Bellwether Media, Inc.

No part of this publication may be reproduced in whole or in part without written permission of the publisher. For information regarding permission, write to Bellwether Media, Inc., Attention: Permissions Department, 5357 Penn Avenue South, Minneapolis, MN 55419.

Library of Congress Cataloging-in-Publication Data
Green, Sara, 1964–
Dalmatians / by Sara Green.
   p. cm. – (Blastoff! readers: Dog breeds)
Includes bibliographical references and index.
Summary: "Simple text and full-color photography introduce beginning readers to the characteristics of the dog breed Dalmatians. Developed by literacy experts for students in kindergarten through third grade"—Provided by publisher.
ISBN 978-1-60014-458-5 (hardcover : alk. paper)
1. Dalmatian dog—Juvenile literature. I. Title.

SF429.D3G73 2010
636.72–dc22   2010000674

Printed in the United States of America, North Mankato, MN.

080110   1162

Contents

What Are Dalmatians?

Have you ever seen a white dog with spots all over its **coat**? It was a Dalmatian! Dalmatians are the only **breed** of dog with spotted coats.

Dalmatians are medium-sized dogs. Adults weigh 40 to 60 pounds (18 to 27 kilograms). They are 19 to 23 inches (48 to 58 centimeters) tall. Dalmatians are in the **Non-Sporting Group** of dogs.

Dalmatian puppies are born with white coats. The spots appear when they are about two weeks old. The spots are usually black or brown. Some spots are as small as a dime.

Some Dalmatians are born deaf. Deafness is more common in Dalmatians than in other breeds.

! fun fact

Deaf Dalmatians can learn to understand people's hand signals.

History of Dalmatians

The Dalmatian breed has been around for many centuries. People are uncertain about its exact **origin**.

8

Ancient images from Asia, Europe, and Africa show spotted dogs. An Egyptian coffin that was made over 3,000 years ago shows the image of a spotted dog!

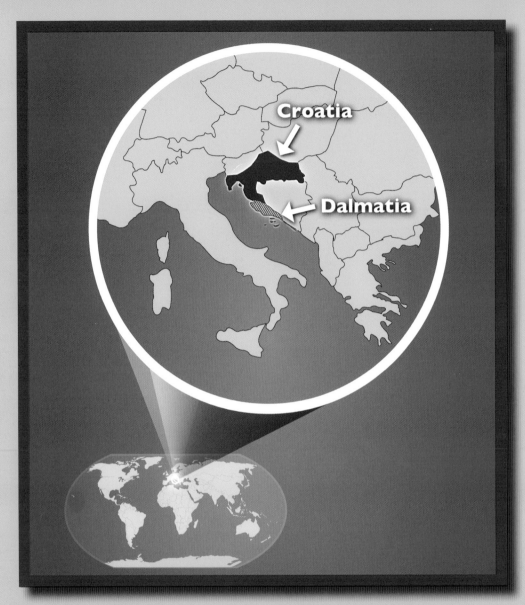

The **Romani people** kept spotted dogs.
They traveled around Europe several
hundred years ago. They brought the dogs
to Dalmatia in the 1700s. Dalmatia is part
of a country now called Croatia.

The people of Dalmatia decided to keep the spotted dogs as guard dogs. People believe that the breed was named after the region of Dalmatia.

Dalmatians also became popular in England. People there noticed that Dalmatians helped horses stay calm. The dogs enjoyed running next to horse-drawn carriages. This was called **coaching**.

Many people used Dalmatians as coach dogs. Dalmatians protected travelers from thieves. They guarded horses and carriages at night.

Early firefighters also used Dalmatians as coach dogs. Dalmatians ran in front of horse-drawn fire wagons to move animals and people out of the way. They also helped out at firehouses by chasing away rats. The Dalmatian breed became the **mascot** for firehouses.

! fun fact

Other nicknames for Dalmatians are Plum Pudding Dogs, Firehouse Dogs, and English Coach Dogs.

Dalmatians Today

Dalmatians do not run with fire wagons anymore, but they still run with horses. Many Dalmatians participate in **Road Trials**. Road Trials test coaching, **endurance**, and behavior skills.

In Road Trials, a Dalmatian runs next to a carriage or horse. A Dalmatian that runs for 25 miles (40 kilometers) and behaves well earns a title called Road Dog Excellent.

Dalmatians also love to hike with their owners. Some owners keep track of how many miles they hike with their Dalmatians. Dalmatians that hike 100 miles (161 kilometers) or more in one year receive an award from the Dalmatian Club of America.

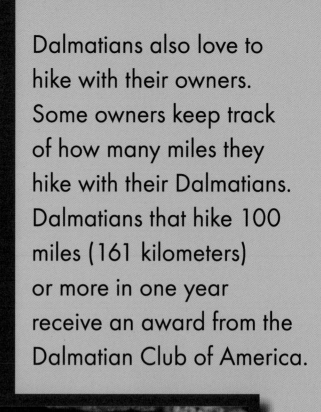

fun fact

Many Dalmatians wear small backpacks to carry supplies when they hike.

Dalmatians are friendly **companion dogs**. Dalmatians smile when they are happy.

They have special muscles in their faces that let them do this. If you are lucky, a Dalmatian may smile at you!

! fun fact

Dalmatians can have blue eyes, brown eyes, or one of each.

Glossary

breed—a type of dog

coaching—running next to a horse-drawn carriage

coat—the hair or fur of an animal

companion dogs—dogs that provide friendship to people

endurance—the ability to do something for a long time

mascot—an animal or person used as a symbol by a group or team

Non-Sporting Group—dog breeds that no longer work or hunt; people keep non-sporting dogs as pets or companions.

origin—beginning

Road Trials—activities that test a dog's skill at running next to a horse or carriage for many miles

Romani people—a group of people that live throughout Europe and Western, Southern, and Central Asia; they are originally from India and left there to travel and settle many different places during the 1100s.

To Learn More

AT THE LIBRARY

American Kennel Club. *The Complete Dog Book for Kids*. New York, N.Y.: Howell Book House, 1996.

Quasha, Jennifer. *The Story of the Dalmatian*. New York, N.Y.: PowerKids Press, 2000.

Stone, Lynn M. *Dalmatians*. Vero Beach, Fla.: Rourke Publishing, 2005.

ON THE WEB

Learning more about Dalmatians is as easy as 1, 2, 3.

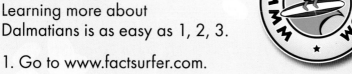

1. Go to www.factsurfer.com.

2. Enter "Dalmatians" into the search box.

3. Click the "Surf" button and you will see a list of related Web sites.

With factsurfer.com, finding more information is just a click away.

Index

The images in this book are reproduced through the courtesy of: Juan Martinez, front cover, p. 21; J. Harrison/KimballStock, pp. 4-5, 8-9; Kathleen Campbell/Getty Images, p. 6; Juniors Bildarchiv/Age Fotostock, p. 7; Jon Eppard, pp. 9 (small), 10; Ron Kimball/KimballStock, pp. 11, 14-15; John James Chalon/Getty Images, p. 12 (small); Utekhina Anna, pp. 12-13; Juniors Bildarchiv, pp. 16-17; Alexander Raths, pp. 18-19; Prue Stuhr, p. 19 (small); Jaume Gual/Photolibrary, p. 20.